Educating for Survival

by Ernest L. Boyer
and Martin Kaplan

Change Magazine Press

Change Magazine Press gratefully acknowledges permission to reprint the following:

Material on page 15 used by permission of *The Stanford Observer*, Stanford University.

Material on pages 20, 26, 27, 28, 31, 32 used by permission of Harper & Row.

Material on pages 26, 35, 46 from *The Search for a Common Learning* by Russell Thomas. Copyright © 1962 by McGraw-Hill Book Company. Used with permission of McGraw-Hill Book Company.

Material on pages 43, 44, 45, 46, 63 used by permission of Columbia University Press.

Material on page 55 used by permission of The Edward W. Hazen Foundation.

Material on pages 59, 60 from *The Purposes of Education* by Stephen Bailey. Copyright © 1976 by The Phi Delta Kappa Educational Foundation. Used by permission.

Material on page 65 by permission of *The Observer*, London, England.

Material on pages 72, 73, which originally appeared in *The New York Review of Books*, from *An Inquiry Into the Human Prospect* by Robert L. Heilbroner. Copyright © 1974 by W.W. Norton, Inc., New York, N.Y.

Material on page 75 reprinted with permission from "Education for Survival" in *Curriculum and the Cultural Revolution*, David E. Purpel & Maurice Belanger, eds. © 1972 by McCutchan Publishing Corp., Berkeley, Ca.

This book was written by Ernest L. Boyer and Martin Kaplan in their private capacity. No official support or endorsement by the U.S. Office of Education is intended or should be inferred. Parts of this book appeared in somewhat different form in the March 1977 issue of Change Magazine.

Foreword

This little book should be welcomed like a houseguest who is long expected but has never quite made it to the front door. What this essay so appealingly reaffirms is the comforting discovery that for every ideological and intellectual movement gone to excess, there must soon come a return swing of the pendulum toward some saner ground.

Nowhere are these wide swings of cultural habit more in evidence than in what is so engagingly called the higher learning in America. With the advent of mass higher education came the cafeteria approach to learning, perhaps an inevitable consequence in view of the large and diverse numbers of students served. But whatever its necessity, it was monstrously wrenched out of focus during the ideological campus wars of the sixties. The snobbish disdain of the children of the upper and middle classes for structure, requirements, intellectuality, and the universities themselves fed still further the almost limitless dispersion of learning content. To this might now be added our new national concern for one's own ethnicity and roots, which splinters what was once considered a common American experience. The resulting microcustomization of the curriculum is more closely associated with cars out of Detroit than with a collegiate experience.

This essay does not deny the necessity of finding our particular cultural antecedents, but it argues that this alone is not enough. It is not the first such appeal for a core curriculum, nor will it be the last. But it is bound to leave its distinctive marks, as it comes at a timely moment in the affairs of this nation. The remains of the seventies and the eighties are likely to produce particularly creative debates about The American Purpose. Educational institutions will inevitably be caught up in this national exercise, as they should be.

Ernest L. Boyer and Martin Kaplan make an ideal collaborative pair for this provocative essay. Education Commissioner Boyer's experience, earlier as a committed dean at small liberal arts colleges and later as head of the country's largest and most complex university system, makes him particularly qualified to speak to one of the central issues in education. His innate social imagination has been suitably tempered by hard pragmatism that comes with the job of a university chancellorship.

Martin Kaplan comes at the issues from another end of the spectrum. His college experience still a recent memory, he is a brilliant and creative humanist, socially concerned without the usual tendency to sermonize. These disparate perspectives of the coauthors have brought them greater combined strengths, and they have recently collaborated in several settings, first at Aspen, then at Cambridge to write this book, and now in government service.

They speak with love and care about matters that have so obviously engaged many a waking hour, and their ideas come to us not as a stranger but as an old friend turning home at last to familiar and comforting terrain.

George W. Bonham
October 1977

I
The Curriculum Has a Core

This two-part essay represents a critical look at the core curriculum in the American college. By "core curriculum" we mean the coursework that undergraduates pursue in common, the cluster of subjects and classes that an institution of higher learning insists that all its students take together. By "critical look" we mean that this book is less a celebration than a diagnosis and a call for action.

A number of assumptions underpin our argument. We have presumed that the college curriculum is a living and evolving part of human culture, the product of history and society; conversely, we have rejected the notion that the curriculum is a value-free, brute fact of nature. We assume that higher learning is a good thing, and we reject the idea that it is merely something else—merely a means of socialization, say, or merely a vocational training ground. We assume the uniqueness of every student and the virtues of pluralism. But we also assume that diversity accounts for only part of our character, that we as individuals also share a common lot and experience.

When in 1974 we began the conversations that led to this book, both of us were in rather different circumstances and surroundings than we find ourselves in now. They deserve a brief recounting here. One of us was the chancellor of the State University of New York, a multicampus system where he had implemented several innovations in educational structures and services—but not yet in curriculum. The other author had been an unsuccessful agitant for undergraduate curricular change at Stanford and was in the process of editing a volume whose title asks the question, What Is an Educated Person? *We discovered in each other a dissatisfaction with what passed for the core curriculum at American colleges and an eagerness to set the right terms of reference for the debate that we sensed would soon break on the American educational scene.*

By the time we had cleared the space to write this essay, the debate had indeed begun in earnest. Harvard—whose Redbook *had been so influential for the American curriculum a generation ago—had issued its "Yellow Pages," the first step in its universitywide attempt toward a kind of* Redbook II. *A Stanford committee, after much discussion, had issued its proposals for a new core curriculum. Amherst and Yale launched similar committees. Symposia on the meaning of the core curriculum in liberal education were sponsored by college associations, by foundations, and by the government. Each month would bring a new article bemoaning the state of the curriculum; each panel discussion or dinner conversation with a colleague would gravitate toward the disrepair of the old common core.*

We were fortunate to have as a setting for this work the University of Cambridge in England, where one of us was a fellow of Wolfson College and the other a returning alumnus of St. John's. The text was put together during a marvelous sabbatical in what may well be the most beautiful university in the world.

At one point in the thick of this work we took an excursion into the English countryside that landed us, one night, reservationless, in the crossroads town of Devizes. The place is particularly undistinguished and would probably be forgotten by now had it not been for two special circumstances. One is that we happened to be there the night of election day, 1976, in the United States. We watched the returns by satellite, in the chilly sitting room above a pub, well into the night and again in the hours before dawn, speculating about the America into which Jimmy Carter's leadership would take us. The other special circumstance came later in the morning. Our bellies full of sausage, chips, and eggs, and our rented car full of chatter about late returns, poll data, and political appointments, we drove across Salisbury Plain to stand in silent wonder at Stonehenge.

Those few days helped put our work on this essay in perspective, orienting it in the most vivid way possible to the past present, and future. We had no idea then that a few days after our return to the United States a series of phone calls would bring both of us to Washington and the Office of Education. We could hardly know in Devizes how closely our futures were linked to those images beamed across the ocean. Though we sensed that morning the dramatic claim that Stonehenge and humanity's past powerfully exerted upon us, we had yet to realize the claims that FOB 6—the Kremlin-like name of the HEW building that houses the Commissioner's office—would stake on our future.

The perspective on the core curriculum from Washington is different in only one key way: The federal government must scrupulously resist legislating the content of American education. But since we have been in the Office of Education, our observations of the national scene have convinced us more than ever that the college curriculum urgently needs attention. We begin, then, with some current observations.

The Educational Stakes

Future historians of higher education will have no difficulty discovering what troubled America's colleges and universities as they entered the last quarter of the twentieth century. Though the metaphors in use today to describe the problem suggest doughboy perils (retrenchment), corsetry (belt tightening, the squeeze, the crunch), and thermodynamics (the steady state), the real topic is absolutely clear: money. It is hunted by administrators, coaxed from alumni, eked out by legislatures, demanded by departments, managed by computers, accepted graciously from students, and eaten by inflation. Money is important, to be sure. The life and death of institutions can depend on it. But balanced budgets are means, not ends. This is why the current university agenda is so forlorn: The educational stakes are so low.

Even utopian solutions to the universities' fiscal woes would not begin to address questions of purposes and priorities. Education for what and for whom? Learning toward what ends, with which curricula, and in what kind of a world? Questions like these give meaning to our money worries; they should set the terms for subsequent tugs-of-war; yet amidst the anxiety of austerity, questions like these are the ones that are barely discussed.

There are, of course, occasional exceptions. It is with one of them that we begin.

Back to Western Civ?

Early in 1976 a Stanford faculty committee issued a report on the Reform and Renewal of Liberal Education. Undergraduate learning at Stanford had last been reviewed in 1969; and following a recommendation of that report, the faculty senate had dropped Stanford's required freshman course in Western civilization. The 1976 committee reversed this stand, proposing that the required study of Western culture be reintroduced.

> The University must introduce students to new areas, ideas, and works, while also providing them with the general informational background and vocabulary of the tradition from which almost all of them come. Moreover, a need exists to reveal the continuity of certain problems and recurrence of some difficulties and solutions to those problems. Stanford graduates must recognize how different historical situations shape what it is possible for people to do and be and must understand what it means to live with traditions different from one's own, with similar traditions, and with no single effective tradition.

Several courses might be used to fulfill the new Western culture requirement, the committee said. These included: a course sequence in Western literature, running from classical to modern times, that "has a long, distinguished history and works from a coherent philosophy"; a history sequence (again classical to modern) taught by the history and classics faculties; a course on theoretic analysis and religious symbolism in the Western tradition, taught by religious studies and philosophy faculty; and an interdisciplinary course in art, music, and drama.

In addition, the committee also recommended a new major—an optional Honors in Liberal Studies program that "declares what in the University's mind constitutes a basis for a sound liberal education." Such a major, the committee said, would be "a congenial middle road between the poles of prescribing what is educationally sound and preserving the student's free choice." Rather than becoming prematurely locked in their specializations, undergraduates might be attracted to the new liberal studies honors major "both because of what it offered and because professional schools would look with favor on their participation," the committee report noted.

The same issue of the *Stanford Observer* that reported these committee recommendations under the headline "Back to Western Civ?" also carried a biting attack on the proposals by the Stanford Associated Students Council of Presidents. The student leaders said that the new report

> proposes to remove from students the right to choose for themselves a course of study. The justification is that many students are too concentrated and others not at all coherent in their choice of classes. Yet that flexibility used to be praised as the advantage of Stanford. The student was free to follow his or her own desires. This is not to deny that courses in Western culture are valuable and that most persons could benefit from them. To require them to take them, however, carries a strong illiberal connotation.... It imposes a uniform standard on nonuniform people.
>
> Innovative curriculum should always be forthcoming. Its quality should be judged not by how many students enroll to complete a requirement but by how many voluntarily take the course, how they review it, and how strong it becomes and remains over time.... Those who wish to take Western culture courses will do so. Those who do not wish to will begrudgingly oblige as they anticipate their liberation from a requirement imposed from above.[1]

With money the leading theme on campus today, we might suspect that the underlying issue in this curriculum confrontation is economic: University administrators, facing dwindling enrollments in "soft" courses, make common cause with languishing humanities departments; a faculty committee calls for departmental subsidies in the form of mandatory courses. Or we might reduce the debate to a sociological squabble: Permissively raised and overindulged students balk at any restrictions on their instinctual drives; faculty and administration retreat to a hopeless nostalgia for the old curricular order. Yet neither of these handy reductions will do. The skirmish over general education at Stanford is important precisely because it exposes issues crucial to the future of higher learning and to the future of society itself.

When the Stanford committee warns that students may become prematurely locked into a narrow field of study, one is reminded that frequently departments are isolated from one another and that students are rewarded by faculty for being promising colleagues-in-the-making. When it suggests that "professional schools would look with favor on [students'] participation" in the new liberal studies major, one recalls that the university has become the hostage of professional school admission committees with their fantasies of the well-rounded candidate. Were today's universities responsive to societal needs and to their own sense of mission, a declaration at this late date of "what in the University's mind constitutes the basis for a sound liberal education" would not be newsworthy. From all indications, the Stanford proposals signal an illness that the core curriculum is meant to medicate.

Symptoms of institutional illness are no less apparent in the students' responses. The name that they give to the freedom to be "too concentrated" or "not at all coherent in their choice of classes" is "flexibility," the flexibility that "used to be praised as the advantage of Stanford." But what institutional model underpins this assessment? What purpose animates an institution that cherishes this all-things-to-all-comers mission? When students say that a curriculum "should be judged not by how many students enroll to complete a requirement but by how many voluntarily take the course, how they review it, and how strong it becomes and remains," are they not merely embroidering on the service station model of the university in which institutional purpose gives way to personal preference?

Finally, when the faculty committee concludes that the new proposal is "a congenial middle road between the poles of prescribing what is educationally sound and preserving the student's free choice," one is tempted to ask, What sort of poles are these? The implication seems to be that university students possess an inalienable freedom, perhaps devolving from their rights as citizens and consumers, and that any attempt to impose upon them an "educationally sound" course of study would violate that freedom. The further implication is that this new major will appeal only to one segment of the motley student constituency; and that this small segment, wooed and won, will reap honors from the faculty as the one group whose free exercise of choice corresponds to the university's declaration of intent. The analogy with television programming—half a dozen network channels ever attuned to market response; one subsidized educational network self-consciously offering quality to a self-selected elite; viewer freedom to twirl the dial—is uncomfortably close.

This blinkered view of student freedom, this turtlelike notion of academic responsibility, and this polarization of the two come down to a curious premise that is suggested in the student council presidents' response. Having acknowledged that Western culture courses "are valuable and that most persons could benefit from them," they go on to say: "To require them to take them, however, carries a strongly illiberal connotation.... It imposes a uniform standard on nonuniform people." It is true that the student bodies of colleges have never been as diverse as they are now. But what is startling is the suggestion that Stanford students have nothing in common with each other and that even to suggest a shared agenda is in itself illiberal. We are indeed islands set apart, or so the students seem to say.

Indeed, if there is a common heritage that unites Chicanos, native Americans, blacks, New York Jews, San Francisco WASPs, Oriental immigrants, ghetto kids, suburban kids, and fundamentalists, then the challenge will be to define it and teach it in a way that transcends the myths of homogeneity and the cultural imperialism of the past. This is not to preclude the possibility of a common heritage but to raise a warning flag. Does coherence include the possibility of radical revision? Does it nurture the creative acts of denunciation and rethinking that have given birth to the identities and images and self-perceptions of cultural subgroups? Will a curriculum that stresses "the continuity of certain problems and recurrence of some difficulties and solutions to these problems" also reveal to students how a nation can become the prisoner of historical images and of the status quo? Will students also learn that the dimensions of "what it is possible for people to do and be" can sometimes serve as political tools? Or in trying to learn "what it means to live with traditions different from one's own, with similar traditions, and with no single effective tradition" will students be drawn inexorably to a cultural relativism that devalues all values and makes a mockery of historical change and human betterment?

We have commented on the Stanford debate and perhaps exaggerated the implications and the distinctions within it not in order to applaud or censure the goings-on but to suggest that any discussion of the general education curriculum will be honest only to the extent that it is also complex. This essay, then, is an attempt to look at what the core curriculum has been and to suggest a new rationale for what it might be now.

Up From Theocracy

Higher education during the whole colonial period was dramatically cohesive. It was bound together by Puritans, morally and intellectually, so much so that the occasional exceptions to the rule—like "witchcraft" and religious dissent—are recalled less for their occurrence than for the stern avenging hand directed toward those who broke the rules. The devotion of the Massachusetts Bay Colony to John Calvin's Christ was reflected in daily life and conduct and extended smoothly into public institutions. The state derived its authority and its rectitude from Christian doctrine. Harvard, the state-church school, received public money to perform services whose purposes were at once religious and intellectual. The production of a learned ministry for the Colony; the creation of an educated class of professional laymen well versed in doctrine; the passing on of the eternal verities of the pagan Ancients and the Gospels—these were the goals of Harvard College with which few would quarrel and toward which the curriculum was organized.

The students were nearly all children of the wealthy—sons of merchants, shopkeepers, master mariners, magistrates, lawyers, gentlemen farmers, militia officers, and, above all, ministers. Only about 10 percent came from the homes of poor farmers, servants, or seamen. Nearly all Harvard students prepared for college by private tutoring, usually from a clergyman, and a thorough knowledge of Latin and Greek was the basic admission test.

Once in the college, all students studied a uniform, rigidly prescribed course that descended, by way of Oxbridge, from the medieval trivium and quadrivium. Classical languages and literatures were continued, and Syriac, Aramaic, and Hebrew were added. Ethics, politics, physics, mathematics, botany, divinity, and metaphysics—their content defined by clerics and medieval scholastics—were also studied in a prescribed sequence. As one history of the period notes, "There was no concept that the varying interests or professional plans of the individual student should be taken into account in constructing a curriculum. It was felt that there was a fixed and known body of knowledge—the 'liberal arts' as they had come down from antiquity via the Middle Ages, Renaissance, and Reformation. This constituted absolute and immutable truth, and it was important that it be absorbed—not criticized or questioned—by every student."[2]

For those early Harvard students and scholars, this tidy curriculum made sense. It was neither the product of petty clerical tyrants nor the instrument of the wealthy to confer intellectual legitimacy on their class privileges—though both of these effects may indeed have been felt. Rather, the fit between the Bay Colony's world view on the one hand and its chief educational means toward those ends on the other was nearly perfect. The Ramist organization of knowledge—descended from Aristotle and modified by Protestant scholasticism—held that the sequence and content of mandated courses reflected a higher order. The curriculum was the intellectual mirror of the divine mind. It was eternal, not subject to revision, and education diligently pursued would lead students to the knowledge of God that was its highest aim. New course sequences, or independent thought, were discouraged or unheard of because tampering with divine wisdom was an impious act. Similarly, classical learning was the sign of gentility, and a thorough familiarity with the wisdom of the Ancients was required in the practice of medicine, theology, and law.

By the time of the American Revolution, some modest changes were in the wind. The American version of Enlightenment democracy had its impact on campus, and in response the curriculum was mildly questioned. Changes were proposed and sometimes implemented. And, throughout the first century of the Republic, secondary education began to shift from clerical tutelage in the classics for the few to broad schooling for the many. The proliferation of Latin grammar schools and the early academy movement—while still far from universal—had their effect. More and more graduates, schooled in more and more subjects, were going on to college. Consequently, the list of required courses began to grow. In 1807, Harvard announced that entering students must be familiar with geography. In 1820, Princeton required English grammar. In 1820, Harvard asked that students study algebra before enrolling, and in 1844 geometry was added. In 1847, Harvard and Michigan put ancient history on the list, and in 1860 Michigan began requiring modern history as well; in the next year, Princeton added English composition as a requirement. This growing entry-level core reflected a changing view of what people ought to know. Perhaps more importantly, it dramatically demonstrated the impact of a growing secondary school system. Philosophical arguments about what entering undergraduates ought to have studied simply could not have occurred without the growth of the lower schools.

Because of burgeoning costs at the oldest institutions, small colleges were founded for poorer students. Their curricular vision, though no less orthodox than that of the more powerful institutions, nevertheless represented a different kind of orthodoxy. These many new institutions with denominational purposes were based on the English model of dissenting academies, colleges newly founded in Britain outside the Anglican orthodoxy mandated at Oxbridge by the Restoration Parliament's Act of Uniformity. In the colonies the new institutions sprouted outside the curricular orthodoxies mandated by the earlier and less tolerant clerics. By 1750, the emphasis of the college curriculum had begun to shift from classics and scripture to astronomy, physics, chemistry, and mathematics.

Two central presences in American society in the century before the Revolution led to proposed (and sometimes implemented) curricular innovations. One, of course, was the democratic ideal of equality. The more populous and diverse the colonies grew, the more it became clear that the educational institutions must serve their diverse needs. Though even the Puritans had expected Harvard to train some lay professionals in medicine and law, their fondest wish was that the College provide a ministry; by the time of the Revolution the careers of Harvard graduates had taken a dramatic turn. Only half the graduates went into the ministry during the first half of the eighteenth century; a decade later this figure had dropped to 37 percent, and at the start of the next century it was a mere 22 percent.

If equality of aspiration was one face of democracy in the pre-Revolutionary period, another was economic growth. The rise of great seaports, of an urban merchant class, of an increasing demand for goods and services—all these led to changes in the curriculum based on new community expectations. In 1749, Benjamin Franklin's *Proposals Relating to the Education of Youth in Pennsylvania* included the idea that there should be a parallel, utilitarian track that students might choose instead of the Graeco-Latin course. In 1753, William Smith—later chosen by Franklin to head a new College of Philadelphia—envisaged in his pamphlet *A General Idea of the College of Mirania* a similar college, with both classical and "mechanic profession" curricula. Where much of American collegiate instruction had occurred in Latin, the Mirania plan called for English. Even within the classical course, subjects would include science, surveying, history, agriculture, English writing and speech, and a kind of contemporary events and issues course "with a view of our colonies in this hemisphere; their state, produce, interests, government, etc., taking some notice as they go along of the French and Spanish settlements that we are chiefly concerned with in trade." Though the College of Philadelphia fell short of the Mirania plan in many ways, it did pare Greek and Latin back to one third of the curriculum; it included agricultural chemistry, surveying, dialing, mechanics, and navigation among the sciences studied; under the rubric of "logic, ethics, and metaphysics," the subjects of political science, trade and commerce, and history found their place in the curriculum; and the reading of contemporary English literature was encouraged.

Throughout the Revolutionary period, Thomas Jefferson, too, pamphleteered for an overhaul of higher education in Virginia. Though his grandest designs went unrealized, he did succeed in shaping a number of changes at William and Mary. The old professorships in divinity and Oriental languages were not abolished, but their influence was greatly reduced. Modern foreign languages, politics, law, economics, and practical and applied arts joined the curriculum.

The stirrings of change could not have occurred without the expanding democratic social climate in the increasingly diverse colonies, without the simultaneous economic development of that fortunate new resource-rich society, without the spread of secondary education, and without the growing number of colleges with different missions. But the curriculum at the American colleges was also being shaped by the larger intellectual revolution.

Earlier ages had been founded on faith, reverence for the past, absolute trust in authority, and the limits of human knowledge. Beginning in Europe about the time of Descartes and reaching its most triumphant expression in the eighteenth century, the world's prior cosmology was shattered as faith was replaced by reason. The validity of knowledge would no longer rest on the unshakable word of the classics or clerics but rather on the empiricism of Isaac Newton. Not only could the validity of scriptural teachings be questioned; one could take the Cartesian mode of doubt as far as the threshold of existence. The certainty of God was replaced by a question mark. And if moral and intellectual verities could be queried and revised, or even exposed and tossed onto the trash heap of progress, so could the existing social realities be held up to scrutiny. Beneath the social structures and the pivot points of power, one searched for rationales; when the rationales were found wanting, other social frameworks were proposed, contracts and constitutions that might in turn give rise to new societies founded on reason and the inquiring mind.

America in the mid-eighteenth century was exuberant with the spirit of the Enlightenment. To get some sense of this, one has only to look at the philosophical issues addressed by her founders and the shape and quality of their arguments. Enthusiasm for reason and for the revolt from dogma spread. The fruits of the new empirical sciences became visible over the whole society, and the general spirit of questioning and skepticism fit the colonies' restlessness with political and religious dogma. The college curriculum was evolving to reflect the society's new intellectual and moral sense of self. Modernity meant more mathematics, more natural (and especially applied) sciences, more English language and literature, more living foreign languages. The changes did not occur, however, without a hearty struggle against the forbidden and corrupting new knowledge.

The Common Foundation of All High Intellectual Attainments

While accommodations occurred following the Revolution, the college curriculum in America generally remained connected to the traditional anchor points of Athens and Calvary. It still stated with confidence what educated people ought to know; it did not shrink from describing how they ought to think and comport themselves; and it had a venerable plan of mandatory study to lead students toward those ends. In fact, to examine college course requirements between the time of the Revolution and the end of the Civil War would lead one to suppose that the Industrial Revolution, the rise of Jacksonian democracy, the conquest of the western territories, the emergence of a native American character and culture, the mounting importance and density of the city, the revolutions in agriculture and experimental science and engineering, and the overwhelming secularization of society were all occurring on some other planet. Or, rather, one might conclude that these social and intellectual upheavals were most deeply felt not by the tiny minority of college students headed toward traditional careers in the ministry, law, and medicine, nor by their professors, but by pioneers and industrialists and farmers and laborers and entrepreneurs too busy or too poor to pay much attention to the niceties of the higher education curriculum. Those who did criticize the traditional college course—for failing to be modern, or mass, or individualized, or American—found their clarion calls generally unheeded.

One such call came from Francis Wayland, president of Brown University, who in 1842 and again in 1855 issued biting criticisms of the American college. The title of the 1855 volume suggests his alternative philosophy: *The Education Demanded by the People of the United States.* He asked that the traditional curriculum be expanded to prepare men to be the farmers and mechanics and great production managers for the future. "Let the college," he wrote, "be the grand center of intelligence to all classes and conditions of men, diffusing among all the light of every kind of knowledge, and approving itself to the best feelings of every class of the community. Let it, besides being a preparatory school to the professions, be a Lowell Institute [a place for technical studies] to the region in which it is placed.... Nothing would so surely annihilate that division of the community into classes, which, already, in spite of our democratic institutions, threatens the direst evils to our republic."[3] In a report to the Brown Corporation, he proposed a curriculum in which "every student might study what he chose, all that he chose, and nothing but what he chose." Well after his program started up and then stopped at Brown, largely because it could not stand on its own economic feet, Wayland continued to hammer away at the need to adapt the curriculum to the changing society. "In a free country like our own," he asked rhetorically, "unembarrassed by precedents and not yet entangled by the vested rights of bygone ages, ought we not to originate a system of education which shall raise to high intellectual culture the whole mass of our people?"[4]

One might fault Wayland's proposal on institutional grounds: It failed to attract a student body; the quality of new offerings fell below the standards of the classical course; and the faculty was largely unresponsive to the idea that responsibility for training students to enter specific careers properly belonged within the college. One might fault Wayland on moral and intellectual grounds: With our comfortable hindsight we see the psychic and social costs of the expansionist economy he so zealously welcomed. But Wayland's proposal rests on a new view of the university's relationship to society, and this is what gives it solidity. In suggesting that the university should open its doors to new groups of students; that its curriculum should be responsive to changing social needs, living within history rather than icily beyond it; and that it extend public and community service beyond the conveyance of information—in all these he laid the groundwork for the diversity and the commitment to equal opportunity that have become the hallmarks of higher education.

The Curriculum Has a Core

But Wayland's plan and proposals from earlier reformers like Thomas Jefferson and George Ticknor posed a threat. An elective system ("what he chose, all that he chose, and nothing but what he chose") seemed to many to undermine the notion of an integrated course of study. It proposed an education that mirrored not God's mind but each individual's wants. What distorted and polarized the debate in the nineteenth century was the failure to recognize that the battles over the curriculum were in fact symptoms of a deeper social conflict. The traits for which the classical curriculum was so admired—its cohesion, its venerability, its acculturative finesse—derived from the homogeneity and gentility of its tiny world of preprofessionals and scholars. It may have been fair to charge that a full elective curriculum was a crass market service with no conceptual center, but the charge was off the mark.

Instead of asking who should attend the university and toward what social ends and then developing an appropriate curriculum consistent with the answers to those questions, participants in the curricular debate approached it as an intellectual question, a battle of the Ancients versus the Moderns. Social needs were ignored. One key document that dramatizes this is the *Report on the Course of Instruction in Yale College* of 1828. "Probably the most influential publication in the whole history of American higher education between the Revolution and the Civil War," as one account calls it,[5] the Report came down hard for a rigid, required curriculum in which only "the thorough study of the ancient languages" could give students the versatile mental discipline necessary to pursue any profession. The college had no proper business in professional training, said the Report; that must come later, after the mental discipline had been acquired and after the student had demonstrated his mastery of the branches of knowledge specified by the Yale faculty that "are the com-

27

mon foundation of all high intellectual attainments." Yale's response to Jacksonian democracy was to fight the battle of populism on the playing fields of Athens.

Yale won. But only for a time, since the Civil War was to shake the American universities even as it did the nation.

We Would Have Them All

The inaugural speech of Harvard's President Charles W. Eliot in 1869 is the classical example of how curricular change is historically determined. The elective system Eliot introduced, says one source,

> met the needs of the American culture of that period. A rural society was being transformed into a great industrialized nation. Keynoting the era were optimism, competitiveness, and materialist expansion. Applied science was more important than ever before. In the realm of thought, it was the age of James's "pragmatism," Dewey's "instrumentalism," and Thorndike's "behaviorism." In such a social and economic structure—in such an atmosphere of thought—the "old time" liberal arts college, with its predominantly clerical administration, its prescribed course founded on an absolute ethics and a theistic faith, and its recitation system, was on the way out. Eliot's elective system, with all its revolutionary implications, was a logical expression of the spirit of the time.[6]

To James, Dewey, and Thorndike, one might add the names of Horatio Alger, Andrew Carnegie, Herbert Spencer, and James McKeen Cattell, America's first professor of psychology; to pragmatism, instrumentalism, and behaviorism, one might append social Darwinism, imperialism, and the newly recognized psychology of individual differences.

Eliot sounded the death knell for the mandatory classical

curriculum. Rather than debate whether the study of ancient languages and literatures was a better route to high intellectual attainment than was the study of modern or useful subjects, he proposed that the curriculum be widened to make room for any topic of liberal inquiry. "The endless controversies whether language, philosophy, mathematics, or science supplies the best mental training, whether general education should be chiefly literary or chiefly scientific," he began his inaugural, "have no practical lesson for us today. This University recognizes no real antagonism between literature and science and consents to no such narrow alternatives as mathematics *or* classics, science *or* metaphysics. We would have them all, and at their best." Having declared the curriculum open, he put Harvard squarely behind the individualistic trend of his time, moving it from a generally prescribed to a generally elective track. By 1895, the only remaining course requirements at Harvard had been pushed back to the freshman year, and even there only two English courses and one modern foreign language were mandatory. Harvard had come a long way from Syriac.

To Eliot's way of thinking, democratizing the curriculum was not an admission that the old unity of knowledge had collapsed or that there was no longer a particular set of courses with which any educated person should be thoroughly familiar. Rather, he held that young men should have "an accurate general knowledge of all the main subjects of human interest, besides a minute and thorough knowledge of the one subject which each may select as his principal occupation in life." If the student could achieve general knowledge, the promise of democracy would be fulfilled. To believe this impossible "is to despair of mankind; for unless a general acquaintance with many branches of knowledge, good so far as it goes, be attainable by great numbers of men, there can be no such thing as an intelligent public opinion; and in the modern world the intelligence of public opinion is the one indispensable condition of social progress." What is so startling about Eliot's proposal is that he assigns this basic education function to the high school. He expected it not only to provide the nation with an intelligent citizenry but also to acquaint the young man with the range of knowledge from which he could pick "what he likes best and is most fit for," his academic specialty and career. Unfortunately, the struggling American public high school system could hardly be counted on to do all this. Worse, the influence of Eliot's ideas was so forceful that when the high school did come into its own, it, too, introduced the elective system.

Laissez-faire in the university meant specialization and intense departmental competition, an aping of the model of the German professoriat. In the end, it was the sciences that triumphed, guided by the hidden hand of capitalism and legitimated by the binding ideology of positivism. The secularization of the curriculum was nearly complete; where once divine law was the unifying logic, now quantification, progress, freedom from set values, and empiricism were dominant themes. Despite the elective freedom for the student to pick and choose from among all offerings, and despite the surrender of the general education function to the secondary schools, the university curriculum had achieved a new, largely unacknowledged integrative principle: the implicit canonization of science, an ideal in tune with the social and intellectual climate.

At the same time, the land-grant colleges were also contributing to the breakdown of the traditional curriculum. Drawing inspiration from Illinois reformer Jonathan Baldwin Turner, these institutions introduced an all-purpose curriculum to serve the practical needs of their communities. "I would found an institution in which any person can find instruction in any study," ran the quote on Cornell's seal. "A state-supported university should contribute directly to improved farming, more efficient industry, and better government," said a leading University of Wisconsin professor.[7] The university should serve the expressed needs of society, and an elective system in a context of diversified departmental specializations was the means to achieve that purpose: This became conventional wisdom by the turn of the twentieth century.

Yet the price paid for giving up general education did not go unnoticed. Though few wished to restore the Ramist axis in the curriculum, many were alarmed by the increasing power of the sciences in the competitive departmental jungle. Though few had the vision or the temerity to propose a new general education design, many wondered whether a compromise between prescription and free choice was possible. The most influential of these was Eliot's successor at Harvard, Abbot Lawrence Lowell, who took office in 1909. In making the distinction between liberal education (the whole of the undergraduate's learning) and general education (the attempt to give one's studies breadth as well as depth), Lowell provided a place for both elective choice and compulsory study. The former could lead to specialization, the latter (at least in theory) to a coherent vision of American commonality, knowledge, and culture. The elective principle, then, gave rise to the major, or field of concentration; here Lowell stressed that mastery of any subject's principles, not only Greek or Latin, would serve to instill discipline, a "strength and soundness of the mental fiber." Toward this end, "all branches of science are good, and so are the various forms of metaphysics and of law. Mathematics is excellent if one has any taste for it, and so are history and literature if they are really well taught." To achieve the "breadth and elasticity of the mind," to become "familiar with the fundamental conceptions that underlie the various departments of human knowledge, and with the methods of thought of the persons who pursue them," Lowell invented the distribution system. Under his guidance, the atomized departments were grouped by a faculty committee into four rubrics: the arts of expression (language, literature, the fine arts, and music); the natural sciences; the "inductive" social sciences; and abstract or deductive studies (mathematics, philosophy, law, social theory). The student was required to concentrate in some elected field and to distribute his other training (roughly half his coursework) among all four rubrics.

But this curriculum was less successful in practice than in theory, a fact worth noting in view of the large numbers of American colleges that have leapt on that bandwagon. In the minds of both students and faculty there arose an inevitable distinction between the seriousness of the major and the comparative fripperies of the distribution requirement; after all, it was the major that was most likely to lead to a career. The various departments united under Lowell's four broad rubrics felt little bond in substance and method and even less in educational mission. And despite Lowell's pleas for general courses under each rubric, satisfying a distribution requirement usually meant taking the introductory course primarily designed for the beginning major (or budding PhD) in the field.

Lowell's balancing act—concentration and distribution—was, as one source notes, at best "artificial. It was only a cross section of courses from specialized and usually unrelated departments. The mere addition or juxtaposition of such courses without any effort at bending them to each other and toward some broad central aim was mechanical at best."[8] Yet what "broad central aim" might there have been? The growth of knowledge, the proliferation of courses in an attempt to win students, and the power of departmental specialization ensured that whatever unity of knowledge was once perceived no longer obtained. Even the power of science, queen of disciplines, had failed to unite the curriculum: Its disengagement from values and its reductive mode of thought had engendered a skepticism so hard-boiled that any curricular unity that survived stood more against than for something.

The disarray within the university was a mirror of the cosmos, shattered so definitively by World War I. The comfortable social cohesion of the past and the intellectual and moral commonality that had underpinned it were being eaten away. Anomie, purposelessness, and hollow individualism replaced them. In the process two key cultures arose. The bourgeoisie, adamant in believing that a new world could be built and founding that belief on the possibility of economic prosperity, was nourished by the specialized tools the university provided for the successful exploitation of the material world. Within its reach were eternal progress and endless growth, and it looked to the university for enough random general intelligence and information to give life a feel of richness and complexity. The other culture, contemptuous of the new bourgeoisie and the society it was building, horrified at the irretrievable wasteland that the moral and intellectual cosmos had become and at the recuperative zeal with which the bourgeoisie was appropriating these cultural shards for its own exploitative ends, arose as the adversary culture we call modernism.

Modernism scored a great success and eventually became a coherent, if tired, culture of its own. On nearly every college campus the names of its poets, painters, and thinkers and its metaphysical buzz words correspond closely to what is regarded as contemporary high culture. But in the society at large, it was the bourgeoisie that held sway, with its exploitation of natural resources, commodity fetishism, unrestrained growth, and purposefully repressive social relations. The poles, of course, were never that sharply drawn. But it is important to bear in mind that the ensuing battle over the general education curriculum took place in the context of this larger struggle.

The Curriculum With a Purpose

The American college curriculum had always been rooted in American social and intellectual life. But in the twentieth century that life was shaken by forces that made prior transformations seem placid. Some of those convulsions might be linked with dramatic public events—the War, the Crash, the Reds, and so on. Other contributing pressures are less vivid but no less real—the emergence of mass society, the alienation of modern life, the collapse of faith in religion and even in rationality. There arose a sense of powerlessness in the face of shattering world events, a readiness to accept discontinuity as normal, a frenetic yen for the new. Perhaps we project some of our own discomfort with today's world onto an earlier time. But even allowing for that, the precipices of the American twentieth century were steep and were scaled not only in the headlines but also in the family, the spirit, the workplace, and the mind. The college curriculum, no less than the individual, had to rediscover its identity in this wondrous and terrible new world.

One new perception of the college's mission drew on the strengths of the land-grant schools and of the elective principle, maintaining that the best curriculum was one that responded best to the needs of its constituencies. The more knowledge there was, the more courses there should be to teach it; the more research money, the more scholars to specialize; the more students to receive the benefits of equal opportunity, the more lecture seats and institutions. Those who felt uneasy about a cafeteria curriculum that invited students to put together their study program the way they did their lunches often followed Lowell's model of compromise: The student should learn a little of everything and a lot of something. With luck, "a lot of something" could be a coherent course sequence providing a solid body of information, rigorous training in skills, and inquiry into the basic principles of the discipline. With less luck, and here the nonsciences stand out, the major became the mélange offered by a particular department whose disciplinary cohesion amounted to "coverage." The "little of everything," in a laissez-faire curriculum with moderate distribution requirements, fared even less well than the major. Departmental offerings were rarely designed for the nonmajor; and when they were, their breathless surveys resembled the highway billboards on the edge of the desert of life: "Last Chance for Eng. Lit." or "Check your Culture Gauge."

It was Lowell's balancing act that most American colleges learned in the early part of the century; the universities made their peace with society by imitating that society. As goes the nation, so go the Harvards. Rhetorical flourishes about liberal learning and versatile education for all life's avenues notwithstanding, this curriculum's rationale was accommodation. And if the intellectual and social life of the time was bafflingly chaotic, what would be the nature of the curriculum that so faithfully accommodated to it? "Intellectual anarchy," answered Archibald MacLeish in 1920. He went on to diagnose the curricular problem this way: "There can be no educational postulates so long as there are no generally accepted postulates of life itself. And there has been no real agreement as to the purposes and values of life since the world gave over heaven a hundred years ago."[9]

Between the time that MacLeish saw the image of the centerless cosmos in the mirror of the university curriculum, and the day before yesterday, a movement was born, flourished, and died in American higher education. Its purpose was to give the lie to MacLeish's charge, and its method was to contradict the drift of modern life with a positive statement of principles, one from which a curricular rationale could be derived. The general education movement, as it was called, was committed to the idea of a curriculum with a purpose. It would be a response to modernism, a counterassessment of the modern world, the universities' therapy for what ailed the society. A core curriculum that offered the minimum indispensables for all educated persons would oppose intellectual anarchy with rigorous cohesion, moral anomie with enlightened commitment, and swarming social heterogeneity with a commonality of heritage and purpose.

Associated with the general education movement are the names of educators like Robert Hutchins, John Erskine, Mortimer Adler, Mark Van Doren, Stringfellow Barr, and Scott Buchanan; and of institutions like the College at the University of Chicago and St. John's College in Annapolis. Ideas differed, of course. Proposals were never purely embodied in curricula, and Chicago in particular evolved its general education program in response to institutional issues not solely tied to postulates about the nature of man and the good society. Nevertheless, this cluster of people and ideas comprises a bright and sharply defined constellation in curricular history.

In the midst of the Depression, an America without a common God was hard pressed to find an ideology to rally round. Communism and fascism had tremendous powers to unite heterogeneous societies. But Americans had no such absolute creed. Democracy, it seemed to some, had become the political face of moral relativism: It had come to mean "anything goes," a loss of nerve, an agreement to disagree. Into this breach stepped the new absolutists, who tacitly held out the hope that American higher education, if only it could rise from the slough of anarchy into which it had descended, could effect a moral, social, and intellectual risorgimento.

These secular absolutists found theological antecedents in the writings of Aristotle and St. Thomas Aquinas. According to the leaders of the general education movement, there are indeed such entities as Absolute Truth and Human Nature; they are susceptible to definition; and from them universal principles of justice and social organization can be derived. Knowledge forms a unity; there are Great Texts of universal and eternal value; "good" and "bad" (in moral judgments) and "right" and "wrong" (in intellectual judgments) have legitimate uses, free of the relativistic fetters of culture, history, economics, or psychology. There are ideas that all educated persons ought to have considered, subjects they ought to have learned, and intellectual skills they ought to have mastered. In such a world, the curriculum is simply the pedagogical embodiment of the wisdom that descends from metaphysical first principles to which all right-thinking persons must agree.

The seductiveness of this way of thinking should be obvious. Under the banner of rationalism, it offers a dazzling synthesis of all knowledge. To those who see a shattered cosmos, it proffers the icons of coherence, certainty, meaning, and purpose. In an insane world it stands against the absurd and for the fructifying and therapeutic power of reason; it proposes legitimate grounds on which to organize social relations and intense ideological commitments. But what should also be obvious are the threats posed by absolute certainty. Though it offers a society based on law and order, it is often the overture to a totalitarian theme. More blood has been spilled in the name of an Absolute Truth than in the service of relatively benign causes like economic imperialism. In the university, absolutism demands approved lists of what every educated person must know. Knowledge must be objective, scrubbed clean of all residues of bias. This extreme of rationalism leads to its own pedagogical tyranny.

The scenario that gives rise to this neo-Thomist curriculum is simple. Once there were absolute and sacred values, and our society and moral life prospered; now, without those gods, relativism prevails; our only hope is a return to the old fixities. It is characteristic of the human mind to approach problems in this way, positing the existence of irreconcilable opposites and seeing solutions only in decisive pendulum swings. Yet another approach, particularly congenial to the American temperament, is solution by synthesis. One sees the two sides of a dilemma and announces that a little bit of both extremes is called for. This eclectic, liberal-minded approach is the informing spirit behind what on all accounts was the most influential document of the general education movement.

The Harvard Redbook

The very first words of the *Redbook*—as the 1946 Harvard report on *General Education in a Free Society* [10] ironically has come to be known—establish the social context in which the report incubated. If the Depression and the threat of potent ideologies had sired an absolutist curricular response, the palpable reality of world holocaust engendered Harvard's response. As James B. Conant said in the opening lines of his introduction, "The war has precipitated a veritable downpour of books and articles dealing with education." In January 1943, in his letter to the Board of Overseers of Harvard College announcing the committee that would produce the *Redbook*, Conant wrote, "Neither the mere acquisition of information nor the development of special skills and talents can give the broad basis of understanding which is essential if our civilization is to be preserved." But if the preservation of "our civilization" was threatened by the Goths without, there was a difficulty to be faced at home as well. "Today, we are concerned with general education," Conant wrote, "not for the relatively few but for the multitude."

The report took pains to stress the triumph of mass secondary education and the concomitant diversity of entering college students—a diversity fed in no small way by the dribbling down of President Eliot's elective system. "The very disparity between students which has forced the high school to its expanded curriculum," wrote the committee, "means that there is no single form of instruction that can reach all equally." The results of this free reign in the high schools were "the alienation of students from each other in mind and outlook because their courses of study for the various diplomas are so distinct, and the disjointedness of any given student's work because instead of being conceived as a whole it falls into scattered parts." Today, mass *post*-secondary education has emerged, based on the elective principle. The committee's observations about the perils of diversity and individualism apply equally to this college sector.

Mass secondary education arose from a commitment to social democracy, and it is within democracy itself that the committee found its central paradox. On the one hand, democracy is tumultuous. Its spirited, ad hoc creativity encourages "exposure to discord and even to fundamental divergence of standards." On the other hand, democracy depends "on the binding ties of common standards. It probably depends more heavily on these ties than does any other kind of society precisely because the divisive forces within it are so strong." Though citizens enjoy freedom to believe differently from each other, without limits to that freedom the democratic society would fail. "It is impossi-

ble to escape the realization that our society, like any society, rests on common beliefs and that a major task of
education is to perpetuate them," the committee wrote,
citing as exemplary and fundamental the beliefs in the
dignity of man, in duty to fellow men, in religious and
democratic traditions, and in the centrality of heritage.
Thus the committee isolated the two poles: democracy's
simultaneous need for creative diversity and for commonality. The problem, then, was to build the eclectic bridge,
to "reconcile this necessity for common belief with the
equally obvious necessity for new and independent in-
sights leading to change."

What follows in the *Redbook* is a series of beautifully
written reiterations of the paradox and of the need for general education to submit neither to the anarchy of laissez-
faire (though democracy requires individual freedom), nor
to the repressions of absolutism (though democracy requires common beliefs), but instead to derive an elegant
and eclectic liberal synthesis. We need to study the past,
but we must not be oppressed by it. We need to inherit
value-laden visions, but we need also to propose our inno-
vative re-visions. "The true task of education," they
write, "is therefore so to reconcile the sense of pattern and
direction deriving from heritage with the sense of experiment and innovation deriving from science that they may
exist fruitfully together, as in varying degrees they have
never ceased to do throughout Western history."
Education "must uphold at the same time tradition and experiment, the ideal and the means, subserving, like our
culture itself, change within commitment." At times, in its
search to formulate the needed reconciliation, the report's
aphoristic prose takes on a gnostic quality. "There are
truths which none can be free to ignore," they write,
playing on the paradox of democratic liberty. "If
toleration is not to become nihilism, if conviction is not to

become dogmatism, if criticism is not to become cynicism, each must have something of the other."

The report says that its recommendations rest on a social fact: "As Americans, we are necessarily both one and many, both a people following the same road to a joint future and a set of individuals following scattered roads as gifts and circumstances dictate." Yet it also rests on an intellectual vision that one of the committee members articulated in an article published that same year. Raphael Demos's "Philosophical Aspects of the Recent Harvard Report on Education" appeared in a 1946 issue of the journal of *Philosophy and Phenomenological Research* devoted entirely to the *Redbook*. Demos drew a sharp line between the intellectual camps that the *Redbook* was attempting to reconcile. On the one side was the party of Heritage; on the other, Change. To the first belonged medievalism, rationalism, unity, a commonality of outlook, and the educational ideals of Robert Hutchins; its excesses, when allowed to flourish unchecked, were traditionalism, indoctrination, *étatisme*, and theocratic dogma. To the other camp belonged the scientific spirit, empiricism, reform, pragmatism, vitality, fluidity, and the educational philosophy of John Dewey; its excesses were patternless anarchy, relativism, and the replacement of cosmos with chaos.[11]

The *Redbook* proposals attempted to embody the liberal synthesis in a particular set of courses outside the departmental offerings. All students would be required to take a course in Great Texts of Literature, a course in Western Thought and Institutions, and a course on principles and methods in either the physical or the biological sciences. These courses would be specially designed to achieve their general education purposes—heritage *and* change, commonality *and* diversity—as would three further mandatory courses chosen by students from a list of upper-division offerings. That the Harvard faculty never adopted the *Redbook* proposals, though they were studied and "implemented" at countless American colleges; that the general education schemes Harvard did try enjoyed an extremely weak institutional position and ultimately languished or died; and that the compromise courses that were adopted rarely lived up to the aspirations of the *Redbook*—all of these considerations, though relevant, prompt one larger question: How valid is the *Redbook*'s rationale? Of what worth is its plan for reconciling what appears to be a fundamental contradiction in democratic society?

The *Redbook*'s diagnosis stands up to scrutiny better than its prescription. American democracy does indeed require both freedom and respect, diversity and commonality, consent and dissent, individualism and community. But as several of its critics point out, the *Redbook*'s strategy simply replaced one problem with another. The Heritage/Change dualism, it said, was bad enough; to "solve" it with a bazaar-like eclecticism only did further violence to the curriculum. The *Redbook*, wrote Sidney Hook, a leading pupil of Dewey's, "ties together incompatible strands of doctrine under the belief it is weaving them into a synthesis.... It rests with the assumption that wisdom consists merely in evenhandedly pointing to the necessity of both elements."[12] Harold Taylor, then president of Sarah Lawrence, wrote, "It is important...in educational thinking not to be bound by the necessity of combining philosophies. The educator is likely to find that by including everything which other educators consider to be true, he will develop an eclectic system whose finished pattern will be conventional, respectable, traditional, and regressive. When we try to find such a pattern, we are in the grip of the rationalistic illusion that there are inclusive systems which can contain contradictory elements. We find ourselves...defending traditional values."[13]

For Hook, only the scientific method (in Dewey's sense) can subsume tradition and change, order and freedom, within itself. For Taylor, Harvard's "synthesis" amounts to a submission to the very medieval rationalism it purported to transcend, whereas only attention to the full development of each student's personal goals can achieve the aims of education in a democratic society. Both critics believe that Harvard's synthesis pays mere lip service to the principle of change, that it really represents a covert alliance with theocratic *étatisme*—hardly a goal for "general education in a free society." The point is put most bluntly in a response to Demos by Horace M. Kallen: "A historian of the future might find himself intrigued by the observation that the insurgence of totalitarianism in the political economy of Europe and the resurgence and advocacy of authoritarianism in the educational philosophies of the United States came at about the same time."[14]

Metacourses

The tension between democracy's needs was reflected in the general education program that evolved at Columbia during World War I. In 1917 faculty member John Erskine proposed a general honors course to confront undergraduates with classic great books, one a week, in intensive discussion sections. At the same time, Contemporary Civilization, "C.C.," the famous history survey that subsequently became the model for Columbia's other general education courses, emerged as a Peace Issues course. It paralleled the War Issues instruction that Columbia gave on behalf of the Student Army Training Corps. The latter, according to Daniel Bell, was established by the government to "propagandize, indoctrinate, and educate" a country divided in its feelings about the war.[15] Columbia's Lionel Trilling later pointed out the inherent tension between the Erskine program, where emphasis on Western classics constituted "a fundamental criticism of American democratic education," and C.C., which was a bald acknowledgment that Columbia had a responsibility to carry out the wishes of that democracy.

It may have been such inherent stresses that led the dean of Columbia in the mid-1960s to ask Bell to propose a scheme for the reform of general education. Bell's report, issued in 1966 on the brink of the worst convulsions ever to grip that campus, received very little attention indeed. But it is the most intellectually rigorous response yet fashioned to the challenge of the *Redbook*, the paradox of education within the context of American democracy.

Bell turns to Trilling for a statement of the paradox. The original strength of the modern secular sensibility was the affront it offered to the established culture, its adversary position toward the suffocating and essentially middle-class values and conventions of the past. Yet modernism itself has become a dominant culture, complete with its convention of automatic opposition. The virtuous tension between the traditional and the new has gone slack because the new has developed a cult of its own which it pursues no less feverishly than the archly conservative society once clung to its traditions. Lionel Trilling asks for a way in which we can "complicate, not retract" the commitment to the modern through the development of a countervailing force. Modernism's radical subjectivity "must be confronted with the mind that insists that...the world is intractable as well as malleable."[16] The university, writes Bell, has become the place where "the tension between past and future, mind and sensibility, tradition and experience, for all its strains and discomfitures," must exist at its most vital.

In this reading, the cultural goal of general education is to keep alive the tension between what we want to be and what we can be, between the claims of the self and the claims of the society. Rather than unifying the curriculum by reference to eternal truths, as do the general education absolutists, rather than falling prey to a benign and befuddled eclecticism, Bell raises the level of inquiry. He will not choose between the medieval and the modern, the canonical and the iconoclastic. He will transcend the poles, asserting that the process in which we deal with ambiguity and paradox is the proper object of study. Less attention should be paid to which truths and values we hold dear or despise, more to the means through which we assess a contention as true or false, regard a value as stale or breathtaking. Truths and values will continue to change, as will lists of great books and ideas and events; the point is not to master the approved lists of the moment but to grasp the crucial and more complex question of how books and events get on a culture's approved list and how it is that they are displaced. As a first step, the college must provide all its students with some basic disciplinary competence. But the next stage is far more important: "the creation of self-consciousness in relation to tradition." Self-consciousness means more than knowing; it means knowing how and why one knows. "It is in this sense," writes Bell, "that the task of education is metaphysics, metasociology, metapsychology, and, in exploring the nature of its own communications, metaphilosophy and metalanguage."[17]

Elements of Bell's proposal hark back to Amherst President Alexander Meikeljohn's 1925 call for a stress not on subject matter per se but on an "analytic course which finds a method of thought and gives a student practice in it." They appear in Brown's Henry Wriston's 1934 call for an emphasis not on course content but on "the essential mode of thought in a field of study, the inherently characteristic mental method of attacking that kind of problem," the "type or category of intellectual experience involved in a successful or fruitful approach to a problem of knowledge." (Wriston's four nominees for categories of intellectual experience were precision, appreciation, hypothesis, and reflective synthesis.)[18] Elements of self-conscious metadisciplines can be observed too in the successive titles of the integrative courses in the University of Chicago's general education program: Methods, Values, and Content; Observation, Interpretation, and Integration; and Organization, Methods, and Principles. To what questions would Bell have students already grounded in preliminary work address themselves? "The limits of empiricism; the nature of theory construction and verification; the nature of explanation and the status of general laws; the distinction between 'cultural sciences' and the 'natural sciences,' between modes of relationships *meaningfully* and *logically* related to each other...and modes of relationships *causally* or *functionally* related to each other, between normative theory and positivist theory; the relation of postulational systems and axiomatic theory to statistical and probabilistic models; and so on."[19]

To achieve these ends, Bell proposed a curriculum organized into four steps. Students would first take a general course sequence in the history and traditions of Western civilization. Second, they would be introduced to a discipline of their choice through special courses in the natural and social sciences. Third would be an extension of that discipline to different subject matter: in effect, the major. Finally, in the senior year, there would be a synoptic program Bell called the Third Tier. Here students would explore the methodological and philosophical presuppositions of their field and apply their specialty to problems requiring a multidisciplinary approach. Courses in this tier would "'brake' the drive toward specialization" through generalization and comparative study. Bell's illustrative titles for coursework in this tier include The Historical

The Curriculum Has a Core

Emergence of the Social Sciences in the Nineteenth Century; The New Nations: Problems of Development; Urban Planning: The Character of the City; Physics and Culture; The Nature of Language; Oriental Civilizations (or Humanities); and Values and Rights.

In a syncretic world, with the volume of knowledge geometrically growing and the functions the university is expected to perform increasing daily, Bell's proposal is a brilliant attempt to contend with the paradox of democracy. Unfortunately, its intellectual triumph is also the beginning of its undoing. How realistic is it to pose metaphysics, metasociology, metapsychology, metaphilosophy, and metalanguage as the central tasks of modern higher learning? The answer depends on who the students are. What lengths of time and depths of talent are required for an undergraduate not only to become broadly educated and to acquire the skills of a specialty but also to engage vigorously both with the assumptions underlying that specialty and with its relations to the epistemologies of other fields? The shift from emphasis on one particular subject to the metaquestions it entails is a superb idea in a world brimming with competing subjects and diverse interests. But some students may be left gasping in the dust.

The old classical curriculum based its commitment to Greek and Latin on a belief in mental discipline and skill transfer that amounted to an empirical claim about how the mind works. The absolutist curriculum derived its core from an empirical claim, too: the permanent, universal truths for which its proponents claimed palpable existence. Bell's proposal, too, implicitly derives from one aspect of reality: the academic department. By shaping the curriculum to the divisions of knowledge sanctified by university disciplines, he has accorded his greatest respect to the institutionalized enterprise of learning. In a sense, this is his answer to MacLeish's query about the purposes and values of life. With an almost Talmudic respect for knowledge, Bell tacitly advocates that we must serve wisdom itself, and that wisdom's crown—its theory and methodology— is the sun around which education must orbit. The beauty and humility of this proposal should not be demeaned. But it is also controversial. If a university is to be responsible not solely to academic departments but also to the world in which its graduates will live, there must be a broader and more urgent mandate for the core curriculum than the philosophy of academic inquiry.

With All the Burdens of Choice

The general education movement, with all its energy and zeal, was short-lived. By the late 1960s it was in its death throes. Though he did not intend it as an obituary, the analysis offered in 1975 by historian William Bouwsma of the various models of "the educated person" held by past societies might well serve as the matching bookend to MacLeish's observations of 55 years earlier. Educational ideals, Bouwsma reminds us, are necessarily relative to the historical contexts in which they are imbedded. What does this imply about any contemporary curriculum that aims to avoid the Scylla of anarchy and the Charybdis of repressive prescriptions? "Any fruitful reflection about the purposes of education," Bouwsma writes, "must now begin with a definition of our own social and cultural condition." He continues,

> We shall need to ask not only what our world is like and what it needs but such fundamental questions as whether it is sufficiently consolidated to permit the formulation of any single educational ideal, whether it is likely to be, or (perhaps hardest of all) whether we really want it to be.
>
> But the relativity of education to its time has a further implication. It suggests the impossibility of es-

tablishing any educational ideal on the cosmic principles that infused some of the most attractive among the ideals of the past. Whether we like it or not, we are, at least for the time being, restricted to a secular conception of education, with all the burdens of choice this implies.[20]

This is not to say that we are without educational ideals. Rather, Bouwsma says, we have too many, and conflicting ones at that, which prevent us from making any choice more decisive than the pluralistic mélange of which Mac-Leish complained. Bouwsma writes:

We face a problem not altogether new but now aggravated beyond anything known before: that we have inherited too much and from too many directions to be able to manage our cultural resources. Thus we now have no classics because we have too many classics. To pose our problem in its starkest and most dismal terms, how can an educational ideal bring into focus a culture that Joyce compared to the scattered debris on the field of Waterloo and that only achieved coherence in his particular vision?[21]

He concludes,

Past experience appears to suggest, then, that any satisfactory educational ideal for our own time must be appropriate to our kind of society and government. If we are to reach agreement about education, we must first agree about the nature of our social and political arrangements, taking into account both their structure and their capacity for change. In addition, an appropriate educational ideal must have some correspondence to our understanding of human nature, its limitations and its possibilities: what it is, what it can be, what it ought to be. These are hard, perhaps impossible questions. But until they are answered I cannot foresee any solution to our difficulties.[22]

The movement in general education represented a series of answers to the challenge posed by MacLeish in 1920 and re-posed by Bouwsma in 1975. In a sense, every scheme developed in the interim—every reply to incoherence—was more than an assertion about the nature of our social and political and cultural arrangements. Each was also a diagnosis of our malady and a regimen for recovery. Ever since the time of Plato, societies have asked that education provide not only instruction in the rudiments but also a knowledge of the good. If today the college seems less a place where values are to be mulled over and reigning ideas assessed, even this briefest look at educational history suggests how marked a departure this is.

General education bears witness to the idea that the university can seek to change as well as to sustain society, can be a fruitful adversary of the dominant culture as well as a supporter, a healer rather than a contributor to the social disease. Our current view of the university as servant of the times may be one reason for the movement's demise. But the failure of general education may have another cause altogether: The countervisions from which these curricula sprang may simply have been inadequate. If that is true, then the movement today remains a potential in search of a proposal.

Since the end of World War II, the chief effort of American higher education has been to extend itself. Access has headed the agenda, and the success achieved is worthy of no small measure of pride. But in this increasingly open setting, progressively less attention has been paid to convergence, to the shared basis of learning that could constitute our universities as communities. What follows is an attempt to reopen the question of the core curriculum and to propose that there is today a basis from which it can be validly derived. In an era when the isolated self dominates our moral thinking, our intellectual culture, our social relations, and our institutional designs, a strong case can be made for a core curriculum based on commonality—commonality in time, on this globe, and together.

Footnotes

1. *The Stanford Observer* (Stanford, Calif.: Stanford University), February 1976, p. 1.
2. John S. Brubacher and Willis Rudy, *Higher Education in Transition: A History of American Colleges and Universities, 1636-1968* (New York: Harper & Row, 1968), p. 13. The exposition in our essay draws substantially on the historical accounts compiled by Brubacher and Rudy and from sources to which we were directed by their extensive bibliography.
3. Quoted in Russell Thomas, *The Search for a Common Learning: General Education 1800-1960* (New York: McGraw-Hill, 1962), p. 22.
4. Brubacher and Rudy, *op. cit.*, p. 105.
5. *Ibid.*, p. 103.
6. *Ibid.*, pp. 114-115.
7. Robert T. Ely, cited in Brubacher and Rudy, *op cit.*, p. 165.
8. Brubacher and Rudy, *op. cit.*, p. 276.
9. Cited in Thomas, *op. cit.*, p. 73.
10. *General Education in a Free Society: Report of the Harvard Committee* (Cambridge, Mass.: Harvard University Press, 1946).
11. Raphael Demos, "Philosophical Aspects of the Recent Harvard Report on Education," *Philosophy and Phenomenological Research VII*:2 (December 1946). See also the other papers in this symposium on educational philosophy: Sidney Hook, "Synthesis or Eclecticism?"; Harold Taylor, "Philosophical Aspects of the Harvard Report"; Claude E. Puffer, "Freedom and Responsibility in Education"; Horace M. Kallen, "Education—and Its Modifiers"; and Raphael Demos, "Reply."
12. *Ibid.*, p. 214.
13. *Ibid.*, p. 228.
14. *Ibid.*, p. 249.
15. This section draws substantially on Daniel Bell's *The Reforming of General Education* (New York: Columbia University Press, 1966).
16. Quoted in Bell, *op. cit.*, pp. 15 and 148.
17. *Ibid.*, p. 152.
18. On Meikeljohn and Wriston, see Thomas, *op. cit.*, Chapter 4.
19. See Bell, *op. cit.*, Chapter 5.
20. William J. Bouwsma, "Models of the Educated Man," *The American Scholar*, Spring 1975, pp. 208-209.
21. *Ibid.*, p. 209.
22. *Ibid.*, p. 211.

II
A Modest Proposal

Can the American experiment survive, in the long run, without exposing our people educationally to their common bonds? Or is it possible to reveal to our citizens, with their thousand varied roots, some core of educational experience that may help assure social continuity rather than further outward dispersion? We believe that social survival in this and the next century is more likely when a common sharing of our human voyage is rediscovered by our educational leaders. We believe that we are indeed in a race for social survival and that some return to a core of learning is crucial to the larger national goals of America's third century.

To build a core curriculum today might seem a hard, almost impossible task. Everything—the vanished consensus, the spread of knowledge, institutional inertia—argues against it.

Yet while diversity necessarily and correctly affirms the individual, education for independence is not enough. Education for interdependence is just as vital. Only a common core of study confronts the fact that isolation and integration are both essential, that social connection points are crucial for greater understanding and survival. Loss of spirit, lack of inspiration, the clash of special interests, the decline of common loyalties—all these must now give way to an awareness based on new global relationships of mutual dependence.

If the history of the core curriculum in American higher education could be set to music, it might sound like this: Proud cadenzas depicting the prescribed classical curricula and the theme of mental discipline would dominate the first movement. To convey the spirit of Eliot's 1869 paean to the free elective system, a darker, more ambiguous leitmotif would be sounded. The Columbia, Chicago, and Harvard *Redbook* scherzo would enliven the next, newly hopeful movement that attempted to find a synthesis between innovation and traditionalism. The final obbligato would perhaps be inspired by the Hazen Foundation's 1968 report on the student in higher education:

> One of the great indoor sports of American faculties is fiddling with the curriculum. The faculty can engage in interminable arguments during years of committee meetings about depth versus breadth. They can fight almost without end about whether education should be providing useful or liberal knowledge. They can write learned books and articles about the difficulties of integrating human knowledge at the time of a knowledge explosion. And of course the battle between general and special education is likely to go on until the end of time. Curricula are constantly being changed. New courses are introduced, new programs offered, new departments are created....
>
> The harsh truth is that all this activity is generally a waste of time.... [1]

The rumbles grow, the hammering noises become deafening, and in the final moments of the cacophony Bouwsma offers a last oracular caution:

> Any fruitful reflection about the purposes of educa-
> tion must now begin with a definition of our own
> social and cultural condition.... Any satisfactory
> educational ideal for our own time must be appropri-
> ate to our kind of society and government. If we are
> to reach agreement about education, we must first
> agree about the nature of our social and political ar-
> rangements.... These are hard, perhaps impossible
> questions. But until they are answered I cannot fore-
> see any solution to our difficulties.[2]

The din closes in over his last words, and the corpse of
general education is at last allowed to rest in peace.

But "our own social and cultural condition" calls out for
a new core curriculum; and while the task of creating one
may be hard, we maintain that it is not impossible. Further, we are convinced that a common educational core
need not mean common repression. The central focus of
our quest is community.

The growth of diversity stands as an honorable component of American history. To claim that our nation is not
one culture but many, to assert the rights of minorities, to
protect individual liberties from mass tyrannies, to protect
the right to dissent, even to disobey—these are all keys to
liberty; and, to the extent that they have flowered in our
midst, Americans may be justly proud.

But this story has an unhappy sequel. Diversity's under-
tow has pulled us far from shore. Democracy requires a
tension between self and society, and yet today the broad-
ening social vision seems in full retreat. The human agenda
that we all confront is global; the issues are transcendent.
Yet social structures are beginning to break apart, and hu-
mans tend increasingly to isolate themselves. Self, pri-
vatism, "your own thing" are the new ruling tides.

Why the excesses of individualism? Some might argue
that a culture founded on conspicuous consumption, on
the acquisition of things, on waste, expansion, and the

manufacture of false needs must come to this social crisis. Others would insist that secularism is the problem. A world without the law and love of God as its guides inevitably will lapse into an unrestrained, self-gratifying quest. But no matter what the root causes, the most urgent task of our democratic society is to invigorate the claims of community while protecting with full vigor the dignity and origins of each individual.

Every core curriculum of the past was guided by the vision of commonality. The classical curriculum that prevailed from the founding of Harvard College to the Revolution was based on the notion of a shared social structure, a communal view as to how all young minds should be trained, and a common belief in God, the church, and the "rights" and "wrongs" that should govern life.

The modest general education reforms from the Revolution to the Civil War, too, did not challenge community. They reinforced it. Science and technology and modern history were added to the curriculum because the society's self-image had expanded, not fragmented. The mental discipline theory held its own because the nature of the mind was biologically and anthropologically determined, not socially variant. The sacred was asked to share its turf with the secular because moral values and ideas of social duty were the common possession of the community, not the invention of the individual. Paradoxically, the race toward free electives was in its own way rooted in commonality: But what was "common" was the freedom of self-determination; what was shared was the right to be autonomous and unique.

The Hutchins model derived from a vision of eternal texts that it is our common obligation to recognize and honor. The Lowell distribution system was based on the logic of academic disciplines and the ways that departments divide the body of knowledge among them; the Bell proposals, by taking aerial photographs of those departments, found a curriculum in the questions common to all disciplines. And when general education languished and died, it was largely because the "commonality" of radical individualism offered a more powerful and accurate image of the times than the alternatives. Individualism was the social fact that earlier social or academic absolutism could not outweigh.

Clearly, students must be free to follow their own interests, to develop their own aptitudes, and to pursue their own goals. On this liberty no one must trespass; this is why colleges have academic majors and electives. But the pursuit of individual preferences is not sufficient. Truly educated persons move beyond themselves, gain social perspective, see themselves in relation to other people and times, understand how their origins and wants and needs are tied to the origins and wants and needs of others. Such perspectives are central to the academic quest.

No single course of study will succeed while all others fail. But to reject a rigid sequence does not mean that a grab bag of electives is the answer, that any academic sequence is as good as any other. General education that focuses on what is shared will not be achieved by accident. To weave such a program into the educational fabric of the college, priorities must be fixed and academic guideposts set in place.

There is, of course, a danger. To insist that individuals temper their demands and negotiate limits to their freedom could mean repression. Calling for sacrifice in the name of some common good may arouse suspicion. But in our own time, with our connecting points strained to their limits, surely constrained self-worship is insufficient. There is today a commonality more urgent and powerful than isolation, and it is this shared human agenda from which the new core curriculum can be derived.

A college curriculum that suggests that students have nothing in common is as flawed as one that suggests that all students are alike. The new common core curriculum is built on the proposition that students should be encouraged to investigate how we are one as well as many; the core curriculum must give meaning, in a democratic context, to *e pluribus unum*. What are these experiences all people share? And which of these common experiences should be studied by the college student? Within the answers to these questions will be found the new common core.

In his provocative new book, *The Purposes of Education*, Stephen Bailey asks, "For Americans living in the last quarter of the twentieth century, what are the bedrock realities of human existence?"[3] He offers three answers. One is that all of us not beset by catastrophe will pass through the aging process—the stages of human development from infancy and childhood through adolescence and adulthood to middle and old age. Second, he says we all decide how we spend our lives. Here he draws an "existential wheel," a pie chart divided into the wedges of work, coping, the free self (an honorific term by which he means leisure), and sleep. The third answer is that all of us live through the various stages of development and spin our existential wheels within the context of a political, economic, and social system.

Under each of these three headings Bailey describes, quite specifically, the content of these "bedrock realities." For example, under the heading of "coping" he lists a lot of activities that occupy adult Americans every week:

> preparing food, eating it, and cleaning up afterwards; brushing teeth; going to the toilet; washing bodies and clothes; shopping, repairing machines (or having them repaired); paying bills; balancing accounts; banking; going to, or worrying about the

need to go to, doctors, dentists, and lawyers; filling out insurance and tax forms; fulfilling mandatory, expected, or hoped-for roles vis-a-vis spouses, children, other relatives and intimates, the community, and the law; parrying the anguishes of self-image, illness, nuclear threats, and relationships with others and with the universe.[4]

From such a police report of how we all log our days, Bailey suggests that education can make a substantial contribution in four key areas: illness, personal and family logistics, psychological misunderstandings, and the search for meaning. But these four topics are less choices from the laundry list of coping activities than headings under which virtually all items can be organized.

Bailey's strategy, then, is to work from the bedrock— life cycle, existential wheel, and enveloping polity—to a statement of educational purposes. When he speaks about colleges and universities, here is how he summarizes the educational missions that are built on the bedrock:

the need for life-long education tied to the predictabilities of stages of human development; the need for increased attention to "mastery skills" to overcome the draining anxieties of existential coping; the need to prepare people for the repetitiveness and routineness of most work, and the importance of creating new forms, modes, and definitions of work; the need to educate people in the negotiating arts, syndetic skills, and moral philosophies of effective political participation in a technologically advanced and structurally ponderous democratic system; and, above all, the need to help people to have truly creative engagements with the taunting and frequently fretful world of the free self.[5]

In strategy, the proposal offered here resembles Bailey's. But it differs in two ways that need underscoring. The first concerns the mission of higher education. It seems self-defeating to suppose that a university, or any school for that matter, is an endlessly pliable institution that can or should do everything. Our society has for quite a while now abandoned the idea that the university acts in loco parentis. But more recently, a service station mentality has had wide currency. In this version, the university is simply what one makes of it, all things to all people. Now this view is being reexamined. The only virtue of recent budget cutbacks may be that they have encouraged renewed debate about institutional mission. Higher education does not have an unlimited number of purposes, nor are those purposes of equal priority. Colleges are beginning to understand that they should not take on responsibilities they cannot fulfill, nor should they attempt to make good on expectations they ought not to have created.

The point is this: What people share should indeed determine what they study together; but not all of what is shared should be studied in the college classroom. Imagine a circle that encloses human beings in all their diversity. Within that circle is a second, smaller one: It contains what they hold in common, the "bedrock realities." But surely this is not the same circle that defines the new common core of collegiate education. That circle is smaller still. Within it are those consequential, intellectually challenging shared experiences that the curriculum appropriately can address. There is no sharp dividing line between circles, nor are their contents frozen permanently. In fact, the common experience that college students should study will be determined by the nature of the university itself— its ability to transmit factual knowledge, its commitment to bring to the surface the value assumptions within arguments, and its recognition that secondary schools have accomplished their own tasks. In this context, then, one must ask again: What is the content of the common curriculum? Which of the knowledge people need in common should the university provide?

Vigilance about university mission is one way in which we differ from Bailey. The other concerns the definition of those aspects of existence that people share. We start here from a different, if anything a more expansive, focus. Our defining premise of commonality is this: We all inherit the past. We all confront the challenges of the present. We all participate in the making of the future. And we all make value choices. The framework of these sweeping, universally shared experiences gives shape and significance to the core curriculum.

We Share a Common Heritage

Colleges have an obligation to help the human race remember where it has been and how, for better or worse, it got where it is. All students must be introduced to the events, individuals, ideas, texts, and value systems that have contributed consequentially to human gains and losses. An understanding of this past from which all of us spring should be required of all students.

This core priority is familiar turf. It sounds very much like general education platitudes of the past, and to some extent it is. But a notion need not be rejected just because it is familiar. The need to acknowledge our heritage is an urgent and ongoing obligation, whatever the fate of earlier efforts toward this end. If colleges do not help keep the past alive and help every student to discover his or her own time perspective, we will not only have lost all memory but bankrupted our future as well.

We need a new approach to avoid some of the pitfalls of the past. It need not be either a breathless rush through the centuries or an eclectic muddle. For example, there may be a dozen or so clusters of ideas and events on which a look at our common past might focus. More than a collection of facts, each cluster might be seen as the convergence of social, political, economic, and intellectual forces. Nor should the label of "history" imply that they are distant, tame, irrelevant. The whole point of looking at our common past is to understand our common inheritance. It is not enough to be told that events have occurred, ideas have been thought, and people have been born and have died. The successful approach will always ask of the past what it has to do with us, how we are shaped by it, in what ways our notions of where we are and what we may become are controlled by our senses of where we were and how we got here.

If this strategy were pushed—and it is offered only to illustrate how to build a core from our common past—then the specific clusters would properly become subjects of debate by all interested groups. Exemplary lists come quickly to hand; here is one proposed by Daniel Bell:

> From tribal to political units; the emergence of the idea of citizenship (from Homer to Solon and Cleisthenes); the Greek city-state (Pericles to the Peloponnesian War); the Roman Republic (Marius and Sulla to Caesar and Augustus); the breakup of the Roman Empire (Marcus Aurelius to Constantine).
>
> Medieval political institutions; the Renaissance and Reformation; the English Revolution; the French Revolution; the nation-state and imperialism; the rise of party systems; the Russian Revolution.
>
> The medieval manor; the rise of cities; the origins of capitalism; the market economy and the price system; the international economy; the modern corporation and the welfare state.
>
> The estate system of medieval Europe; the challenge of equality—religious and secular; rationalism and empiricism and their social bases; the industrial revolution and the breakup of traditional society: from status to contract; social classes: bourgeoisie and working class; critiques of modern society; bureaucratization and professionalism.[6]

Such a list is neither final nor exhaustive. For example, Bell leaves the history of science for another portion of his curricular proposals, but some observers might consider it essential. What dozen or so moments are the most crucial to inherit? The criteria would surely include the density of the moment (the way it serves as a magnet for social, economic, political, and intellectual forces); the degree to which it represents the crystallization of a historic characteristic (e.g., the neoclassic) or a historic transition (e.g., Newton); and the way in which that moment radiates out to include ourselves.

Such a list is not comprehensive, but we believe that no attempt should be made to worship the deity Coverage. After all, the lower schools and reference works still serve as resources for continued learning. One could do worse than to learn less about world history and more about the world. Perhaps it may be fruitful to sacrifice the traditional survey material of colonial history in order to include a three-week case study of the Salem witch trials. To choose a few things carefully; to study them intensively and across disciplinary lines; and through them to see our own times—these goals may be adequate for the new core.

And here a special word of caution: A chief danger of any study of the past is that we come to believe that our current view of things is the only accurate one and our description of history is an improvement over past accounts. We tend to forget that the very different senses of what in the past is of lasting significance—senses held by other ages and cultures and even by various communities within our own culture—deserve to exist in hearty competition with new notions of what the great events and ideas are. No less important than inheriting a vision of the past, then, is learning about re-vision, a universal process crucial to understanding historical change.

Thus a component of the core curriculum's approach to

heritage should be concerned with change, with shifts of historical paradigms, with sets of events viewed from different vantage points. One might study how the conventional wisdom about American involvement in Indo-China changed from 1950 to 1975. One might compare visions of Communism, or of time, in the 1920s and 1970s. One might trace how the ideas of empire, colonization, and "manifest destiny" were born, implemented, and radically revalued. One might look at a particular historical moment from the perspective of black people, or of women, or of non-Western cultures. One might draw inspiration for case studies from an account like the following excerpt from Patrick O'Donovan's column in a 1976 London *Observer*. It was written on the occasion of British publication of a contemporary Russian textbook account of World War II:

> History is seldom written as a deliberate lie, and this must be kept in mind when reading a history of the last war as taught to Russian schoolchildren.... History must be tinged with ideology, with the love or the hatred of one's own country. It cannot be utterly objective. The French and the English have cohabited since the time when they were not even nations. The histories they teach their children are different and the differences go far deeper than the different interpretations of the Battle of Waterloo.
>
> Between ourselves and the U.S. there are spectacular differences in what is taught as history. The war of 1812, for example, is hardly known to us; to the Americans it is not only the time when the British burned the White House but when an American warship could be almost certain of beating its British equivalent.
>
> The most spectacular difference in the interpretation of history in the West probably occurs in Northern Ireland. The Catholic and Protestant school histories might be about different countries and they play a creatively divisive role there.[7]

Finally, no look at the common and changing past would be complete without a look at the most traditional idea of commonality enforcing our historical inventory, the concept of human nature—its limits and its possibilities. The common core should investigate the ways in which human beings are intractable as well as malleable, always taking care to be self-conscious about the origins of ideas about intractability. Individuals are unique and also belong to concentric circles of communities: Students should be asked to consider the forces on all sides and how the balance has changed. Are there fixed limits to what can be expected of a society? Are all people necessarily selfish or warlike? Are human capacities set anthropologically and psychologically, or does one's historical perspective play a special part in establishing the realm of the possible? Questions like these need to be addressed in any attempt to relate human history to the history of inherited self-images.

We All Confront the Challenges of the Present

Here is a curious fact: General education proposals have almost always focused on past traditions but have been remarkably inattentive to the commonality in the contemporary world. The new common core should ask students to look at the contemporary world and to understand the processes in which, as social creatures, they are engaged.

Symbols are central to existence. So fundamental that it is often overlooked is the fact that people are socially bound together by the sending and receiving of messages through sight and sound and touch. The process is mutual and essential. It goes far beyond the personal need to learn to write and speak clearly and connectedly, learning to decode the messages of others. We are, in fact, bombarded by signals—exhorting us to think, live, feel, believe, and act in certain ways. Our knowledge is embodied and conveyed in symbols. Our internal conversations with self, and our communications with others, are all mediated by the complex miracle of language—language in the broadest sense. That we are all inhabitants of a linguistic space is the rationale for including an approach to communication in the common core.

All students should be exposed to a broad range of issues raised by our common existence in a world of messages. They should have an awareness of how languages develop, of the symbols we use, of the process of receiving and interpreting messages, of breakdowns in communication, of the search for an international language. They should strive for "comprehensive literacy"—an ability to spot the hidden presuppositions behind an act of communication, to infer the intent and suasive designs of a message. They should, for example, learn how to deal critically with advertising and propaganda; by looking at television news, they might elaborate a notion of "tube literacy." Students should also be developing an awareness of symbol systems other than English. Mathematics, computer language, dance, foreign languages, music: A grasp of languages such as these, besides having intrinsic worth, can illuminate the many ways in which messages can be encoded, decoded, distorted, or shared.

We are shapers of institutions and are shaped by them. Living in modern society means interacting with institutions. Understanding our common plight means developing institutional literacy; no educational enterprise has done its job if it has not acquainted its students with the roles, rights, and responsibilities of the principal institutions—public and private—that make up their world. The core curriculum, then, should survey key sectors of American life, sectors whose presence is ineluctably felt by all: government and law, business, finance, the economy, and the private nonprofit realm. How institutions in these sectors have developed, what functions they perform, to whom they are accountable, how they respond to social change, how they interrelate: Topics like these should be considered.

Case studies would be particularly useful adjuncts here. If their angle of approach were determined by an insistent issue in the news—"ungovernability," national health insurance, balance of payments, the charitable deduction—so much the better. To look at the way in which institutions have been built and reshaped does not mean the resurrection of civics courses, though the changing notions of citizenship would of course be explored within any approach to institutions. Nor need this approach mean a souped-up economics course, though a certain amount of economic description and theory would doubtless be included. The guiding logic should be common membership in a polis whose institutions all members are meant to serve and be served by. What explicit and tacit social contracts people have made with those institutions and how they can renegotiate the terms are issues at the heart of the rationale.

We all produce and we all consume. For too long colleges have neglected the ways in which society is defined by the common activities of getting and spending. Except for a handful of individuals, no one can choose not to work; and everything we know about society suggests that work choices are overwhelmingly important in shaping the values, culture, and social relations of a time. In an era when "rampant preprofessionalism" is alleged in nearly every quarter; when the liberal/vocational dichotomy arouses intense debate; and when nearly 95 percent of undergraduates in poll after poll rate training and skills for an occupation to be important goals of their education—in such a time, no stronger mandate is needed than our inescapable faith that we are "workers together" for the university to think more carefully about the meaning of work and the need for students to understand that meaning.

The common core would acknowledge the powerful influence the university itself has in shaping the work choices of its students. Such a curriculum would broaden perspectives by asking: What have been the historical, philosophical, religious, and social attitudes toward work around the world? How does work relate to the fundamental value choices that every student must confront?

We hear a lot of talk about liberal versus vocational education, and it is suggested that the collegiate tradition of formal education is demeaned if it seems to lead directly to a job. But such a view distorts the present and denies the past. If the truth be told, education from its earliest days has been introduced and defended precisely because of its practicality, because of what it has prepared students to do. Harvard College, in addition to defending the Christian faith, was launched to prepare young men for the ministry, law, medicine, and other honorable professions pursued by the privileged. In more recent years, arts and sciences majors were in fact practical preprofessional sequences intended for those planning to go on to graduate school, teaching, and research. The assumption made by even the most avowedly "liberal" colleges has always been that one would move on to a productive job; the greatest failure of a department occurs when its graduates cannot "get placed."

Work is not dishonorable, and educators do a great disservice to suggest to students, even covertly, that it is. Work is universal; it tells a great deal about people and cultures on a very personal level. For many of us work is an expression of who we are and where we fit. "I work, therefore I am" may be an overstatement of the case, but it touches a circumstance familiar to us all.

Education, while its purpose must always go beyond work (and this is the quarrel with the narrow vocationalists; work, not education, is their goal), does not and should not bypass the centrality of work—historically, culturally, and personally. If education cannot relate to that part of human life devoted to productivity—even, at times, creativity—then it has failed most fundamentally.

It is often argued that some work is not vocation, that some jobs are not uplifting but degrading. This is true, of course, and the circumstances surrounding that fact should also be carefully studied. But our problem of relating work to higher education cannot be so easily dismissed. The truth is that many new kinds of useful, challenging, even crucial jobs have emerged, and yet educators still confer prime legitimacy on those that have been around since time immemorial. Tradition, lethargy, ignorance, and snobbery have led teachers to make mindless distinctions between what is legitimate and illegitimate for students to plan; such distinctions have led to equally mindless choices about what can and cannot enter the curriculum. It is all right, some say, for a student to prepare to be a doctor, but it is less all right to be a nurse. It is all right to be an engineer, but a computer programmer is suspect. Teaching college is just great, but teaching elementary school is something else again. To dig ruins of the past is a respectable objective, but to plan to work with ruined lives in an urban jungle—a more complicated and demanding venture—is not so worthy. To read what has been written in the past is just fine, but to aspire to write about the present is not legitimate at many arts and sciences colleges.

What logic is used by those who make distinctions such as these; those who guard so arbitrarily the vocational portals; those who, by the curriculum they offer, determine for students what work is honorable for the educated person and what work is not? The time has come to give a new objectivity, a new dignity, to work of all kinds; to recognize that college graduates, instead of being demeaned by all but the status professions, can in fact lift up a job and give it new meaning, while giving their own lives new meaning as well. Past attitudes have propped up a class system to ensure that those in the educated class were also in the high-salaried, status-job class. This new emphasis on work and its meaning is not to urge that colleges become vocational; rather, it is to suggest that they rediscover the true meaning of liberal education.

We Are All Making the Future

That human beings inherit a common past and inhabit a common present will seem controversial to few, but to advance the truism that they have a common future as well is to startle the curriculum from a millennial slumber. Yet, there is no sharp distinction between the future and the past and the present, and educators have failed in helping students grasp this fact. Nothing raises the question of interdependence and community existence more crucially than the tomorrow which, willfully and willy-nilly, is being made today.

As we see it, then, the future must be a part of the curriculum to be studied. If consideration of the past and present emphasizes American society's internal connectedness, looking ahead will underscore complex global interrelations. And to inquire about that is to wonder not only whether the future will resemble the present but also whether there will be a future. The easy confidences with which Americans have lived—the beliefs that we shall go on getting richer, healthier, brighter, and shinier—seem less and less adequate foundations on which to build. Future alternatives, and the critical choices they pose, must be closely observed, above all by those who will live a large portion of their lives after the year 2000.

But how is the future something to be studied? Where does one begin? One approach must be to build models of the future—the future based on what is known today. Some observers say that air and water will continue to be polluted. The exponential depletion of natural resources will not be checked, nor matched by a commensurate new technology of methods for harvesting energy and raw materials. The proliferation of nuclear weapons, particularly among the less developed nations, could lead to war, or at the very least to an unsteady succession of threats, crises, and international blackmail. Overcrowding and massive starvation, coupled with drought and an inability to produce sufficient quantities of the right kinds of food, will take their phenomenal toll. A change in climate, perhaps the melting of the polar ice caps due to the heat blanket of the earth's atmosphere, could be disastrous. Social unrest on a national and global scale may well be directed against the unequal distribution of wealth. Moneyed interests and the powers of science and technology may be perceived as encroaching on the individual's freedom and quality of life.

Such a dismal view is taken, for example, by Robert Heilbroner in his volume *The Human Prospect.* "There is a question in the air," he writes, "a question so disturbing that I would hesitate to ask it aloud did I not believe it exists unvoiced in the minds of many: Is there hope for man?"[8] Heilbroner's visions of the future may or may not be overly apocalyptic, but they make clear that it is no longer possible to assume that some cosmic United Fund has guaranteed the future. Global destinies, once having arrived collectively at some irretrievable, unmanageable point, cannot then be reversed to some earlier moment of sanity.

Heilbroner writes,

If, then, by the question, Is there hope for man? we

ask whether it is possible to meet the challenges of the future without the payment of a fearful price, the answer must be: There is no hope.... The human prospect is not an irrevocable death sentence. It is not apocalypse or Doomsday toward which we are headed, although the risk of enormous catastrophes exists. The prospect is better viewed as a formidable array of challenges that must be overcome before human survival is assured and *that can be overcome* by the saving intervention of nature, if not by the wisdom and foresight of man. The death sentence is therefore better viewed as a contingent life sentence—one that will permit the continuance of human society, but only on a basis very different from that of the present, and probably only after much suffering during the period of transition. [9]

The point to emphasize here is Heilbroner's phrase "the wisdom and foresight of man." He looks pessimistically at the possibilities of deploying those venerable faculties, and perhaps his position is a sound one.

There are other views, of course, based on different assumptions and drawing inquiries from different data. The point is not to promote one future view but to discover the interrelationships between what people do today and the lives they will live tomorrow. What we are proposing, then, is a twenty-first century version of general education that draws on the wisdom of the past, organizes our present knowledge of the world, and then focuses sharply on alternatives for the future. Education, indeed, has no higher ethical commitment than to provide students with a thorough value-laden preparation for the next century.

Another approach to the future was suggested by Gus Tyler, assistant president of the International Ladies' Garment Workers' Union, in his article "Everybody's Core Curriculum." "Between 1970 and 2000, the top item on mankind's agenda will become survival of the species." He continues:

As a dark age descends, our institutions of higher learning may choose to reenact their medieval role as keepers of the candle; in which case, they are likely to exist with the rest of us. Or they may choose to remake themselves to confront the challenge of human extinction; in which case, both the universities and mankind may be reborn as more viable entities....

Let there be a core course on Survival of the Species (SOS for short). Its object would be, first, to make each of us aware of our common peril....

Making survival the prime *raison d'être* of higher education could breathe new life into the curriculum, inspiring urgency and relevance in both the hard and soft sciences. Students in search of involvement would find fresh motivation. Faculty could come out of their cloistered cubicles and be joined by more teachers drawn from that alien and less alienated world outside the classic walls. And the institution would find that the outsiders on the campus would be inside the civilization. [10]

The university's role in survival, though, should not be construed solely as a technical exercise designed to craft the political and environmental strategies that will save us. Rather, the study of the future should involve these acts inherent in all scholarship: the search for enduring values, the exposure of hidden assumptions, and the confronting of value-laden choices.

Educators need to look first at a subject whose existence is too rarely acknowledged: the history of the future. In many ways societies are held together by their images of the future. It is important to consider the images of the future that earlier cultures have possessed, as well as to look more closely at utopian literature, science fiction, scripture, millenarian tracts, and other sources of such images. Who are the social prophets of our time? What images of the future does our society possess—what are its central dogmas and how do these compare with the forecasts offered by the emerging profession of futurology? And how does the process of policy planning translate future alternatives into current choices?

It will not be enough, though, to confront the future solely on this broad basis. Intensive case studies of problems already upon the world should stress participatory responsibility in making the future. The span of topics might be suggested by this list, adapted from Michael Scriven's "survival curriculum":

> Abortion; censorship; police review boards; euthanasia; cities; nationalization of foreign-owned industry; unionism; sumptuary laws; "equal time" on television; subsidized art; radioactive and industrial waste contamination of the earth's water supplies; the economics of power production; the magnitude of the pest and parasite problem in food production and storage; the existence and probability of antibiotic-resistant strains of staphylococcus and bacteria which would defeat medical advances; the limited size of our coal reserves; the knowledge explosion and the data-storage and retrieval problems it creates.[11]

Each teacher surely has other nominees, but the point is that problems of the future—that is, problems of the contemporary world—deserve a firm place in any new core curriculum based on commonality.

Past, present, and future: Humankind's rootedness in time has suggested the components of the new core. But there is one theme that cuts across time and also gives definition to a common identity. The theme has, by implication, been repeatedly addressed within our proposals for the core, but it is of such universal significance that it also deserves a focus of its own.

We Are Partisans; We All Make Ethical Choices

As a capstone to a core curriculum, we propose a very strong and forward look at the moral and ethical considerations that guide the lives of each person, a kind of forum in which personal beliefs could be discussed. Everyone "believes," everyone continually makes value-laden choices, and no one holds values wholly unrelated in origin and impact to the values held by others.

For too long colleges and universities have suggested to students that beliefs are somehow less important than "the facts." But regardless of the pretensions of its member disciplines and the magisterial rhetoric of the college catalogs, the university—in its every procedure, structure, requirement, option, budget detail, admission, promotion, publication, grade, syllabus, and diploma—acts out the choices and commitments it has made. None of these choices is "natural." All are human-made, subject to revision, born of values, inherently controversial, and rooted in time and place and economy and faith.

The core curriculum must make such an acknowledgment about the university, about each person within it, and about the world. It must encourage frank and searching discussion about the choices people make and why they make them, about religious beliefs and ideologies. It must bring students into contact with people who hold explicit ideals, people outside the university, people who can talk carefully and thoughtfully about their own commitments and who are capable of pursuing questions like, When should values change? When should partisanship be revised?

In this way, the core could even become a forum for its own self-examination. What are the assumptions from which other approaches to the core have arisen? What presuppositions underlie a free-elective system? What tenets give rise to an approach based on commonality? Such questions could provide an occasion for frutiful revision of the rationale and content of the core.

Most visitors to London will have strolled along Charing Cross Road and browsed in the used-book shops that crowd its sides. Dilapidated volumes (and occasional treasures) are shelved floor to ceiling and often spill out into sidewalk stalls and boxes. Not long ago, riffling through one of those boxes, we discovered a little treasure: *Essential Knowledge for All* it was called in proud gold capitals stamped on the red spine. On the title page—opposite an etching of an aquiline Man holding Earth between his hands at cerebrum height and captioned, "Knowledge itself is Power: Francis Bacon"—appeared the forthright subtitle, "A MODERN AND AUTHORITATIVE OUTLINE OF THE ESSENTIAL BRANCHES OF KNOWLEDGE FOR ALL WHO SEEK TO BE WELL INFORMED." Its 500 pages offered an encyclopedic look at the world—seen from Britain in 1946, the same year the Harvard *Redbook* appeared. We found chapters by a dozen hands, organized under titles like Art of the World, The Solar System and the Stellar Universe, Main Currents in World History, and Economics in Theory and Practice. The first chapter, The Pattern of Knowledge, was exuberant with the potentials of wisdom and of the record of humanity's accomplishments. "Knowledge," it read,

> is a totality that has emerged by the united effort of mankind. There is a oneness or unity about it. Each generation learns its particular lesson from its own experience, just as each individual does. He works, thinks, feels—and what he learns he passes on to his children and his neighbors. It drops into the common pool, becomes a tradition in the household, in the family, in the workshop, the factory, or the office. It

finds its way into conversation, into letters, into books, into schools and colleges. It spreads outwards through the community like ripples on the surface of water. Each generation inherits the best of past experience. Each generation climbs onto the shoulders of the last and looking back can survey with clearer vision what has been accomplished.[12]

And optimistically it proceeds in this vein with a clear message: The book's covers enclose a distillation of world wisdom, a core curriculum, as it were, for the hip pocket.

The nobility of that goal is not totally undercut by the specter of its dusty remains tossed in a box of near discards in Charing Cross Road. Humanity has never been embarrassed by its hope that the best of which it is capable can be selected and passed on; democracy has never given up the dream that this best can be made available not to a select and homogeneous few but to the diverse many. So here, we have maintained that the movement away from the required classical core and toward do-it-yourself electives has been informed by, and has contributed to, the hypertrophy of individualism. We have proposed instead a new core curriculum based on the irreducible commonalities of our existence. There must be some humility in such a gesture; after all, academic schemes, too, have their own Charing Cross Roads to receive their weary bones. Yet without the hope that there is some common pool to which all peoples contribute and from which all are obliged to draw, there is also little hope for together coming to terms with the world that the colleges are allegedly preparing the next generation to inherit.

To attempt to provide a sturdy pair of shoulders onto which the diverse individuals of the future may climb might appear at this late hour a quixotic enterprise. Still, we have made the necessary wager here that it is not yet impossible. To suppose that the task is archaic is one

A Modest Proposal

thing—an erroneous supposition, in our opinion. To suppose that it is hopeless is bluntly unacceptable.

Footnotes

1. Committee on the Student in Higher Education, *The Student in Higher Education* (New Haven, Conn.: The Hazen Foundation, 1968), pp. 35-36.
2. William J. Bouwsma, "Models of the Educated Man," *The American Scholar*, Spring 1975, pp. 208-211.
3. Stephen Bailey, *The Purposes of Education* (Bloomington, Ind.: Phi Delta Kappa, 1976), p. 3.
4. *Ibid.*, pp. 27-28.
5. *Ibid.*, pp. 110-111.
6. Daniel Bell, *The Reforming of General Education* (New York: Columbia University Press, 1966), pp. 221-222.
7. Patrick O'Donovan, *The London Observer*, November 14, 1976, p. 13.
8. Robert L. Heilbroner, "The Human Prospect," *The New York Review of Books*, January 24, 1974, p. 21.
9. *Ibid.*, p. 33.
10. Gus Tyler, "Everybody's Core Curriculum," *Change*, May-June 1970, pp. 51 and 55.
11. Michael Scriven, "Education for Survival," in *Curriculum and the Cultural Revolution* edited by David E. Purpel and Maurice Belanger (Berkeley, Calif.: McCutchan, 1972), pp. 172-173.
12. Hyman Levy, F. Sherwood Taylor, Harold Spencer Jones, *et al.*, *Essential Knowledge for All* (London: Odhams Press Limited, 1946), p. 6.

**For a free catalogue of other
Change Magazine Press
publications, write to:**

Change Magazine Press
NBW Tower
New Rochelle, N.Y. 10801